party food
for girls

party food
for girls

Alessandra Zecchini & Arantxa Zecchini Dowling
photography by Shaun Cato-Symonds

NH
NEW
HOLLAND

First published in 2011 by New Holland Publishers (NZ) Ltd
Auckland • Sydney • London • Cape Town

www.newhollandpublishers.co.nz

218 Lake Road, Northcote, Auckland 0627, New Zealand
Unit 1, 66 Gibbes Street, Chatswood, NSW 2067, Australia
86-88 Edgware Road, London W2 2EA, United Kingdom
80 McKenzie Street, Cape Town 8001, South Africa

Publishing manager: Christine Thomson
Editor: Louise Russell
Design: Sarah Elworthy

National Library of New Zealand Cataloguing-in-Publication Data

Zecchini, Alessandra.
Party food for girls / Alessandra Zecchini & Arantxa Zecchini Dowling;
photography by Shaun Cato-Symonds.
Includes index.
ISBN 978-1-86966-299-8
1. Holiday cooking—Juvenile literature. 2. Quick and easy cooking—
Juvenile literature. 3. Baked products—Juvenile literature. [1. Holiday cooking.
2. Quick and easy cooking. 3. Cooking. 4. Baked products.]
I. Dowling, Arantxa Zecchini. II. Cato-Symonds, Shaun. III. Title.
641.568—dc 22

10 9 8 7 6 5 4 3 2 1

Colour reproduction by Pica Digital Pte Ltd, Singapore.
Printed in China by Toppan Leefung Printing Ltd, on paper sourced from sustainable forests.

contents

introduction

I recently observed my 12-year-old daughter Arantxa and her friends organising the food for a birthday party and I was impressed with their creativity and attention to detail. But I also realised that they didn't have much in the way of resources to draw upon.

What would an ideal party cookbook contain for them? And for a parent?

I talked about it with Arantxa and we decided to take up the challenge. We worked out that the cookbook should teach some basic skills, but mostly should provide a lot of inspiration, freeing the imagination to create something unique. So, once we have mastered a basic recipe – for pizza, say, or for cupcakes – we have the ability to create something new every time.

A party cookbook should contain some healthy recipes that are good for growing kids, but also sweet recipes. Everything in moderation!

And, of course, let's not forget about style! Most girls love to develop their own style, are well informed about fashion and trends and are very interested in colours and presentation.

Finally, a few words about skill. You don't need to start with skills, as these develop quickly with practice. What generates talent in the kitchen is a confident approach to learning. If learning to cook and to prepare food is made to be fun, and is supported by happy results, it leads the way to becoming a confident cook.

Arantxa and I developed, prepared and styled all these recipes together, and we hope that the following pages will inspire you and make your next party a success.

Alessandra Zecchini

pretty cupcakes &
fancy toppings

in this first chapter we start with some fun projects: making the prettiest cupcakes and the fanciest toppings! The recipes are very simple, and some have been further simplified to be suitable for younger readers and first-time bakers. Cupcakes can be easy to make because of their size, they don't require a long time in the oven, and by using paper cases you won't risk them sticking to the baking tin. Also, you don't need to worry too much about their look: with a few decorating tips (such as the frosting and icing techniques given here) you can transform even the plainest cupcake, and later on the simplest biscuits and cakes, into delectable treats.

vanilla dream cupcakes

An easy recipe, and one of Arantxa's favourites, that always gives perfect results and makes the prettiest cupcakes ever.

for the cupcakes
120 g butter
3 eggs
130 g sugar
1 teaspoon vanilla essence or vanilla paste
200 g self-raising flour
60 ml milk

for the topping
Italian butter icing (see recipe on page 22)
fresh or sugar flowers (see recipe on page 71) to decorate (optional)

Preheat the oven to 175°C. Line a 12-hole muffin tray with paper cases.

Melt the butter in a jug, either in the microwave or in the oven (while the oven is warming up for the cupcakes). Place the eggs and sugar in a mixing bowl and whisk, using an electric beater, until the mixture looks light and pale yellow in colour. Slowly add the melted butter and the vanilla essence or paste. Keep beating at a low speed; add half the flour followed by half the milk. Add the rest of the flour and milk and keep beating, making sure there are no lumps. Divide the mixture between the 12 cupcake cases.

Bake for about 18-20 minutes, until golden brown on top. You can also check readiness by inserting a toothpick into a cupcake: if it comes out clean, the cupcakes are ready. Remove the cupcakes from the tin and let them cool down.

Prepare the Italian butter icing and decorate as you wish.

makes 12 cupcakes

tips & variations

You can decorate these cupcakes with fresh edible flowers like violet or rose petals, if you like. Make sure the flowers haven't been sprayed. You can also buy edible flowers in the salad department of some supermarkets. Remember: if you are not sure about a flower, do not eat it! Sugar flowers can be bought from cake-decorating shops, or you can make your own (see recipes on pages 13 & 71).

rose cupcakes with sugar rosebuds

For these lovely cupcakes we have used the basic vanilla dream cupcakes recipe and moved towards a more exotic taste and romantic look.

12 vanilla dream cupcakes (see recipe on page 10)

for the sugar rosebuds
cornflour to dust your hands
white, pink, yellow and green fondant or rolling icing

for the icing
6 tablespoons icing sugar
1 tablespoon rose water
1 tablespoon water
3 drops blue or red food colouring (optional)

Make the sugar rosebuds first, at least 2 days before the cupcakes.

Dust your hands and fingers with cornflour. Take a small amount of white fondant and roll into a ball as small as a pea. Roll it with your finger into a little sausage, lightly flatten, and then roll it up to make a rosebud. Repeat until you have 12 white rosebuds. Next, do the same with the pink and then the yellow fondant, until you have 36 tiny rosebuds. Now take a small amount of green fondant and, with your fingers, roll it into very small strips, to resemble long rice grains. Set aside in a cool, dry place, but don't refrigerate.

Make the icing by mixing the icing sugar with the rose water, adding a little water if necessary to reach the right consistency. Add food colouring, if using, and mix in well.

Turn the cupcakes upside down and dip them into the icing. Hold them upside down for a few seconds to let the excess icing drip off and then quickly turn upright. Let the icing set a little and then repeat, adding a second layer of icing. If your cupcake case is quite large and the top very flat you can add the icing with a spoon, if you prefer. Finally place 3 little rosebuds and a few green 'leaves' on each cupcake. Let the icing set before serving.

makes 12 cupcakes; sugar rosebuds: dairy free, wheat free

tips & variations
You can also use the sugar or marzipan roses from page 71 for this recipe, or add some fresh rosebuds (only as decorations, not to be eaten). If time is an issue, use ready-made sugar roses from a cake-decorating shop.

berry & cream cupcakes

Everybody likes berries, and they are perfect for decorating your cupcakes. If you want to put the cupcakes in your lunchbox, leave out the cream and fruit. Just by themselves they will taste delicious! Even younger readers can make these simple cupcakes.

for the cupcakes
120 g butter
3 eggs
130 g sugar
200 g self-raising flour
60 ml milk
6 teaspoons berry jam (any kind)

for the topping
300 ml cream
1 tablespoon icing sugar
fresh berries to decorate

Preheat the oven to 175°C. Line a 12-hole muffin tray with paper cases.

Melt the butter in a jug, either in the microwave or in the oven (while the oven is warming up for the cupcakes). Place the eggs and sugar in a mixing bowl and whisk, using an electric beater, until light and fluffy. Keep beating and slowly add the melted butter, followed by the self-raising flour and the milk. Mix well, making sure that there are no lumps, and then divide the mixture between the 12 paper cases. Drop half a teaspoon of jam on top of each cupcake and bake for about 18-20 minutes, until golden brown at the top. You can also check by inserting a toothpick into the cupcakes; if it comes out clean the cupcakes are ready. Remove the cupcakes from the tin and leave to cool.

When the cupcakes are cold, whip the cream with the icing sugar and pipe over the cupcakes. If you don't have a piping bag, use a spoon or a spatula to decorate your cupcakes. Top with fresh berries of your choice.

makes 12 cupcakes

tips & variations

If you use the same kind of berry jam and fresh berries you can change the name of this recipe, for example: blueberry cupcakes, strawberry cupcakes, and so on. Instead of the cream topping, use Italian butter icing (see recipe on page 22) if you prefer.

tips & variations

These cupcakes are quite sweet and rich, so probably don't need any more sugar decorations. However, to add a touch of colour, cut out some pretty patterned paper in whatever shape you like and glue them over toothpicks to make little flags. Otherwise, just top with a fresh cherry or strawberry.

chocolate truffle cupcakes

The perfect cupcakes for chocoholic girls and their mums! Make these for St Valentine's Day, Mother's Day, birthdays or other special occasions that call for chocolate.

for the cupcakes
50 g dark chocolate
100 g butter
100 g sugar
3 eggs
1 drop pure vanilla essence
200 g self-raising flour

for the topping
chocolate ganache (see recipe on page 25)

Preheat the oven to 175°C. Line a 12-hole muffin tray with paper cases.

Melt the chocolate with the butter, either in the microwave or in the oven (while the oven is warming up for the cupcakes), then whisk with an electric beater. Add the sugar, keep beating, and add the eggs one by one, the vanilla essence and the flour. Divide the mixture between the 12 cases and bake for about 18–20 minutes. You can check if the cupcakes are cooked by inserting a toothpick into them; if it comes out clean the cupcakes are ready. Remove the cupcakes from the tin and leave to cool.

Prepare the chocolate ganache. Refrigerate the ganache for 1 hour and then whip with an electric beater until it doubles in size. Spoon the mixture into a piping bag with a medium or large nozzle and pipe onto your cupcakes.

makes 12 cupcakes

birthday cupcakes with fondant icing

These cupcakes are perfect for birthdays, and they can also be used to make a cupcake cake. The base is the same as the chocolate truffle cupcakes, but the topping is made with ready-made fondant icing and . . . a little creativity.

12 chocolate cupcakes (see recipe on page 17)
2 tablespoons apricot jam
cornflour to dust
1 packet white fondant icing
food colouring (optional)
icing pens (optional)

Prepare the cupcakes and, when cool, brush the tops with apricot jam.

Sprinkle a little cornflour over a clean, dry bench and a rolling pin and roll out the fondant icing. You should aim to have a 1 cm-thick icing.

Using a cup or round cookie-cutter, cut 12 discs big enough to cover your cupcakes. Place carefully on top of cupcakes.

Squash together the leftover fondant. At this point you can choose to colour your fondant with 2–3 drops of food colouring (or more drops to make a brighter colour), or leave it white. Roll out to 1 cm thick. Use a small knife or cookie-cutters to make fondant flowers or different shapes, for decoration. Alternatively, use icing pens to decorate your cupcakes.

makes 12 cupcakes

tips & variations

You can arrange the cupcakes on a cake stand or pile into a pyramid shape on a serving plate, and add candles – one for each cupcake if you're turning 12!

plum cupcakes

These soft and fruity cupcakes are made without butter or milk, so they're suitable for those who need to avoid dairy products. You can use this basic recipe for many more cupcake variations, with or without fruit.

for the cupcakes
200 g plums
120 g sugar
3 eggs
180 g self-raising flour
60 ml vegetable oil
zest of 1 lemon

for the icing
runny icing (see recipe on page 29)
1 drop red food colouring (optional)

Wash the plums and cut into small pieces, removing and discarding the stones. Set aside. Preheat the oven to 175°C. Line a 12-hole muffin tray with paper cases.

Place the sugar and eggs in a mixing bowl and beat, using an electric beater, until light and fluffy. Add the self-raising flour and mix. Slowly add the vegetable oil and then the lemon zest. Keep beating at a low speed until all the ingredients are well mixed, making sure that there are no lumps.

Fold the plums into the mixture. Divide the mixture between the 12 paper cases.

Bake for about 20 minutes, until the cupcakes look cooked. You can also check for readiness by inserting a toothpick into the cupcakes. If it comes out clean, the cupcakes are ready. Remove the cupcakes from the tin and let them cool down before icing them.

Make the runny icing. Add red food colouring (if using). Turn the cupcakes upside down, holding them with your fingers, and dip them into the icing. Hold them for just a few seconds to let the excess icing drip off and then quickly turn them upright. If you like, add a small slice of plum to the top of each cupcake. Let the icing set before serving.

makes 12 cupcakes; dairy free

tips & variations

You can substitute cherries or berries for the plums. You can decorate your cupcakes with sugar flowers or fruit. It is also possible to bake your cupcakes in ovenproof china cups greased with oil.

Italian butter icing

This is an almost-professional soft icing, the sort that makes the tall, airy swirls on cakes in fancy cake shops. Save your pocket money to buy a piping bag with different nozzles, and practise making lots of swirls and shapes on your cupcakes. It is so much fun!

160 g unsalted butter
2 egg whites
160 g sugar
10 ml water
a few drops of pure vanilla essence

Cut the butter into small cubes and set aside at room temperature.

Beat the egg whites with an electric beater until they form a peak, then add 100 g of sugar and beat for 10 more minutes.

Put the remaining 60 g of sugar into a small saucepan. Add the water. Place saucepan over a very low heat and bring to the boil. Simmer for 2 minutes, stirring gently with a metal spoon, and making sure the sugar doesn't stick to the edges of the saucepan. The sugar should melt but still look white. Don't boil it for too long or it will turn into brown caramel, or dry up into a solid lump. If this happens, wash the saucepan with warm water and start again.

Resume beating the egg whites and very carefully (don't burn yourself) pour in the sugar syrup. Beat until the mixture is cold and then turn the speed of the beater to the lowest setting. Add the butter, little by little, and beat until well mixed. Add the vanilla essence and beat for one more minute.

Scoop the icing into a piping bag and decorate the cupcakes as shown.

makes icing for 12 cupcakes;
wheat free

tips & variations

For coloured icing, add a few drops of food colouring after putting in the vanilla essence. If you don't have a piping bag, spoon the icing directly onto the cupcakes (or cake) and smooth it with a spatula or a knife.

chocolate ganache

This is another fantastic topping, which can be used to decorate cupcakes, as a filling for biscuit sandwiches and to coat cakes before adding fondant icing. This recipe provides three different types of topping.

200 g dark chocolate
100 ml cream

To melt the chocolate you will need to use a bain-marie. Place a metal or Pyrex glass bowl over a saucepan filled with water. The bowl should be a little bigger than the saucepan, so that no water or steam can escape and ruin the chocolate (or burn you!). Cube the chocolate and place inside the bowl with the cream. Slowly bring the water to the boil and simmer, stirring constantly with a small hand whisk or a spatula, until the chocolate is melted. Remove from the heat, taking care with the hot water and escaping steam. Keep stirring the ganache as it cools down.

For a lighter, airy topping (top):
Refrigerate the ganache for 1 hour, then whip with an electric beater until it doubles in size. Spoon the mixture into a piping bag with a medium or large nozzle to decorate your cupcakes or cakes.

For a rich, truffle-like topping (centre):
Refrigerate the ganache for 1 hour and then spoon into a piping bag with a medium nozzle to decorate your cupcakes or cakes.

For a smooth and shiny topping (bottom):
Spoon a little ganache, still warm, directly over your cupcakes or cakes.

makes icing for 12 cupcakes or a 20–25 cm cake; wheat free

tips & variations

You can make ganache using milk or white chocolate, but it becomes rather sweet. We find dark bitter chocolate is best suited for this purpose.

easy royal icing

Royal icing is perfect for decorating special cakes and creating outlines before flooding biscuits with coloured runny icing (see recipe on page 29). Traditional royal icing can be quite hard to work with. This version is softer and easier to handle for younger cooks, but it will still set into a hard, meringue-like icing.

1 teaspoon cornflour
200 g icing sugar
1 egg white
1 teaspoon lemon juice

Sift the cornflour into the icing sugar and set aside.

Place the egg white in a mixing bowl and whisk with an electric beater until soft peaks form. Keep whisking and add the lemon juice, followed by the icing sugar, one spoonful at a time. Whisk until sugar is well mixed in and the mixture looks shiny. Spoon into a piping bag and decorate your cakes or biscuits as you wish.

makes icing for 12 cupcakes, a 20–25 cm cake
and approximately 30 biscuits; dairy free, wheat free

tips & variations

This icing hardens very quickly. Either use it immediately, or cover with some plastic food wrap. Do not refrigerate. This icing can be coloured, but it looks better white. For a chocolate version, add a teaspoon or two of cocoa to the mixture when whisking in the icing sugar.

runny icing

This icing will provide a smooth and perfect coating. Because it is egg white-based rather than water-based, it will harden more quickly and is particularly suited to decorating biscuits.

1 egg white
1 teaspoon lemon juice
8–10 heaped tablespoons icing sugar

Place the egg white in a mixing bowl. Add the lemon juice and one heaped tablespoon of icing sugar. Stir with a spoon (this time do not use an electric beater. You are mixing, not whipping the egg white). Continue adding the icing sugar spoon by spoon until you get a white icing, which should be runny, but not watery. You will need 8-10 tablespoons of sugar, depending on the size of your egg white. Always have some icing sugar on the side in case you need more, and if the icing becomes too thick add a teaspoon of water to thin it down.

Spoon the icing directly onto your cake or biscuits as you wish.

dairy free, wheat free

tips & variations

You can add food colouring to this recipe to make coloured icing. Divide the icing into smaller containers and add a different colour to each one for a range of different-coloured icings. This icing sets quite quickly, so use it immediately or cover well with a lid or plastic food wrap until you're ready to use it. Do not refrigerate.

party food & finger food

with so many things to think about when you are planning a party — from the music to the right things to wear, from the invites to the decorations — you may feel that you don't have much time left to dedicate to the food. But remember, after all the chatting and dancing, your friends are soon going to get hungry. Plus, party food is fun to make! Here there are lots of ideas, some of which won't take much time at all, and some that don't even involve cooking, just assembling. And in the Tips & Variations boxes you will find more ideas for making food to suit your party theme.

Italian party skewers

The ingredients here are just a suggestion for what you might choose when assembling your own party skewers. This is a fun project to do by yourself or with your friends.

12 long wooden skewers
12 small squares of focaccia bread (about 3 cm thick)
12 basil leaves (optional)
12 pitted green olives
12 bocconcini (small mozzarella balls) or any other
   white cheese, cut into small cubes
12 red cherry tomatoes

Thread the following onto each skewer: a piece of focaccia bread, a basil leaf, an olive, a small mozzarella ball or piece of white cheese and a cherry tomato. Make sure to leave some space at each end of the skewer for easy handling. Place the skewers into a tall vase, so that they can stay upright, or lay them on a serving plate. Spiking the skewers into a whole raw pumpkin or a big bread loaf also looks impressive.

makes 12 skewers

tips & variations

Make international party skewers by using different kinds of breads and cheeses. You could try: brown bread and Emmental cheese for a Swiss theme; mini pita and feta cheese for a Greek theme; pieces of baguette and Camembert for a French theme, and so on. Make little flags for each country out of paper and different-coloured pens, then stick them to the end of each skewer.

petit fours for classy parties

Have you got a special occasion coming up? Maybe it's a wedding or an engagement, a new baby or a naming ceremony and you would like to help. These petit fours are easy to assemble and look very sophisticated.

ready-made Madeira cake
runny icing (see recipe on page 29)
a few drops of food colouring (optional)
sugared almonds to decorate

Cut the Madeira cake into little rectangles, about 5 cm long, 4 cm wide and 3 cm high. Place the cake pieces on a cooling rack over a clean tray or a sheet of greaseproof paper.

Make the runny icing and colour it if you like, using just a few drops of food colouring. With the help of a spoon pour the icing over the miniature cakes, covering all the sides well. This takes time. If the icing is too thick, add a teaspoon of water and mix in thoroughly to thin it down.

Place a sugar almond on top of each petit four and let the icing set for a few hours. Put aside in a dry place away from the direct sunlight until serving time, but do not refrigerate or the icing will liquefy.

makes approximately 20 pieces

tips & variations

Do not use sponge cake instead, as it will be too crumbly. However, you can use fruitcake, if you prefer. In fact, fruitcake is perfect with white icing and white sugared almonds to celebrate a wedding, engagement or Christmas. To celebrate a new baby, you could use pastel pink icing for a baby girl and pastel blue icing for a baby boy.

giant pasta shells

You can buy giant pasta shells from most delis and specialist food stores. They can be eaten as finger food – warm or cold – with a variety of fillings. Pasta is easy to make and pleases most palates – it's a safe bet when Arantxa's friends are staying for dinner.

20 giant pasta shells
salt
6 tablespoons finely chopped cooked spinach
200 g soft feta cheese
fresh edible flowers and herbs to decorate (optional)

Boil the giant pasta shells according to packet instructions (with a little salt added to the water), then drain and rinse under cold water until they're cold. In a bowl, mix the spinach with the feta until you have a creamy mixture. Fill each pasta shell with a little mixture and place on a serving tray. If you like you can decorate each shell with an edible flower or fresh herbs.

makes 20 pasta shells

tips & variations

These pasta shells can also be heated up under the grill or in the microwave. Serve about 5 or 6 per person as a hot dish.

cheese & capsicum open sandwiches

This is the perfect recipe for a party tray, and a change from the usual club sandwiches.

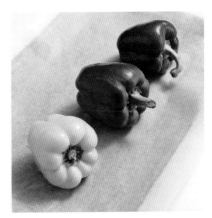

3 capsicums (1 red, 1 yellow and 1 green)
6 slices wholemeal sandwich bread
butter or margarine to spread
6 cheese slices

Preheat the oven to 200°C. Place whole capsicums on a baking tray lined with baking paper, and roast for 20 minutes.

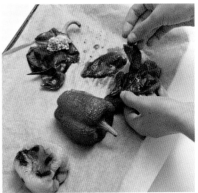

Turn the capsicums over and bake for a further 10 minutes. Turn the oven off and leave the capsicums to cool down inside the still-hot oven. After 1 hour take the capsicums out of the oven and remove the stalks, seeds and skin. This job is a little messy, so do it over a bowl or in the sink.

Place the capsicum flesh on a chopping board and, by using small cookie-cutters or icing cutters, make 12 or 24 colourful shapes. Set aside.

Cut off the crusts from the bread, then spread bread with butter or margarine and cut each slice diagonally to make two triangles.

Cut each cheese slice in the same way and place a cheese triangle over each triangle of bread.

Top the open sandwiches with a cut-out piece of capsicum (or two if you have made 24) and serve as canapés.

makes 12 pieces

tips & variations

Rather than using processed cheese slices, use fresh Edam or Maasdam cheese slices (available in most supermarkets). If you need to save time you can also buy slices of capsicum already roasted.

stuffed cherry tomatoes

This dish is perfect for little fingers and artistic girls who like miniature food and details. Offer to make this when your parents are having a party – everyone will love them.

20 cherry tomatoes, not too ripe
2 tablespoons chunky pesto dip (or any other dip you like)
chopped fresh herbs to decorate

Using a small knife, cut the tops off tomatoes and empty them of their seeds so that they become little hollow containers. As you work, place the hollow tomatoes upside down on a chopping board or tray, so that any remaining liquid drains out.

Carefully fill the cherry tomatoes with the dip (you won't need much) and arrange on a tray or serving plate. You can put the tomato 'tops' back on like lids, or decorate the open tomatoes with chopped herbs.

makes 20 tomatoes; wheat free

tips & variations

Use both red and yellow cherry tomatoes to add colour.

For an even simpler dish, just fill the cherry tomatoes with a tiny piece of fresh mozzarella, and decorate with small basil leaves.

individual mini pizzas

Pizza is the ideal party food. This recipe has been tested over and again by Arantxa, her brother and their friends during some awesome pizza parties (see Tips & Variations below).

for the pizza dough

300 ml warm water

2 ½ teaspoons active dried yeast

¼ teaspoon sugar

500 g high-grade or strong flour, plus extra for dusting

1 large pinch of salt

for the topping

1 x 400 g can chopped tomatoes

100 g grated mozzarella cheese

dried oregano to sprinkle (optional)

salt to taste

2 tablespoons extra virgin olive oil

fresh basil leaves to decorate

tips & variations

Make a pizza party: provide some ready-made dough and a selection of toppings and ask your friends to create their own pizza.

Put the warm water in a large mixing bowl and add the yeast and sugar. After 5 minutes, when the yeast starts to bubble, add the flour and salt then work into a dough for another 5 minutes or so. You can knead it directly on the table or in the mixing bowl. Shape the dough into a ball, sprinkle it with a little extra flour and leave to rise in its bowl, covered with a tea towel, for about 2 hours.

Punch the dough and knead it for 1 minute, then divide it into four equal parts and then divide each part into three smaller balls. You should get 12 small balls. Put these on a floured surface, dust with flour and cover with a tea towel. Leave to rise for 30 minutes.

Preheat the oven to 200°C. Take the dough balls and one by one flatten them into small circles, using either your hands or a rolling pin.

Place the circles on an oven tray lined with baking paper. Top each one with some chopped tomatoes and grated cheese, then add a sprinkle of oregano, a pinch of salt and a drop of olive oil. Bake for about 12-15 minutes, until the borders of the pizza look cooked. Taking great care not to burn yourself, remove the pizzas from the oven and decorate with fresh basil leaves. Serve hot or cold.

makes 12 mini pizzas

grissini

Your friends will love nibbling grissini, the thin Italian bread sticks. This is one of the easiest grissini recipes – you just need to bake them twice to make them crispy.

400 g high-grade or plain flour
1 pinch salt
250 ml warm milk
2 teaspoons active dried yeast
¼ teaspoon sugar
4 tablespoons extra virgin olive oil

Place the flour and salt in a large mixing bowl and make a hole in the centre so it resembles a volcano. Fill the hole with the warm milk, then add the remaining ingredients to the milk and start mixing all the ingredients together with your fingers. Mix for about 10 minutes, until the dough is quite elastic, then shape it into a ball. Cover the bowl with a tea towel and leave to rise for 1 hour.

Line a baking tray with baking paper and preheat the oven to 200°C.

Take a small piece of dough and roll it into a breadstick around 20 cm long. Lay it on the baking paper. Repeat until the baking tray is full of breadsticks and then bake for about 25 minutes, or until the grissini are golden. Remove from the oven, let them cool down, then bake a second time for 5-10 minutes more, so they become crispy.

makes approximately 30 grissini

tips & variations

For a sesame or rosemary variation you can add a tablespoon of sesame seeds or chopped rosemary leaves to the risen dough. Mix the dough well and then roll the grissini as directed in the recipe.

verrines

'Verrine' means food layered into a glass or a small glass bowl. Generally starters or desserts, verrines look very fancy because of their colourful layers. In fact, they are very easy to make, as these next two recipes will show.

berry cream verrine

100 g frozen mixed berries
1 tablespoon lemon juice
2 tablespoons sugar
300 ml cream
500 ml ready-made custard (or see recipe on page 51)
12 strawberries
extra fresh berries to decorate

Place the frozen berries into a bowl, add the lemon juice and sugar and set aside for 1-2 hours, stirring from time to time. Strain and collect the juice. Whip the cream until high and soft, and fold half into the custard. Slowly add the berry juice to the other half of the cream and fold to make a pink cream.

Hull and cut the strawberries into 2 or 4 pieces (depending on their size) and divide between 6 glasses (8 if using small flutes). Top with the mixed berries. Slowly spoon the custard on top, working lightly so that it doesn't go through the berries (ruining the layer effect). Finally, top with the pink cream, using either a spoon or a piping bag. Garnish with fresh berries. Refrigerate until serving time.

makes 6–8 verrines; wheat free

tips & variations

If you use very tall glasses you can make even more colourful layers, for example: adding green kiwifruit and/or rockmelon cut into small cubes between the custard and the cream.

fruit salad verrine

1 x 400 ml can lychees
1 medium slice watermelon
4 kiwifruit
½ rockmelon or honeydew melon

Drain the lychees, keeping aside the liquid for later use.

Cut the watermelon into 2-3 cm pieces and divide between four tall glasses (like those used for ice-cream sundaes or cocktails. Shorter glasses are also fine, as long as you can assemble the fruit into layers).

Peel and cut the kiwifruit into 2-3 cm pieces and place over the watermelon.

Place the lychees over the kiwifruit.

Peel the melon, remove the seeds and cut into 2-3 cm pieces. Place the melon over the lychees.

Add a little liquid from the lychees to each glass. Refrigerate for at least 30 minutes.

Serve with a fork or long wooden skewers to help pick up the fruit.

serves 4; dairy free, wheat free

tips & variations

You can use whatever fruit you want here. Just remember to alternate colours so that you have a nice visual effect. If you wish to use apples and pear slices, soak them in lemon juice first so that they won't turn brown.

bigné

Bigné are small choux pastry shells filled with a sweet or savoury creamy filling. In this recipe we use light custard, and then whipped cream and fruit for a luscious and colourful ending.

20 ready-made choux pastry shells
300 ml cream
1 teaspoon icing sugar
fresh fruit to decorate

for the custard
1 egg
2 tablespoons sugar
1 tablespoon flour
250 ml milk
1 drop vanilla essence

Make the custard first. In a small saucepan mix the egg and sugar with a wooden spoon. Place the saucepan over a low heat, add the flour and mix well. Add the milk little by little, making sure it doesn't form lumps, and bring to a gentle boil. Simmer, always stirring, until the custard is ready, about 8-10 minutes.

Stir in the vanilla. Leave the custard to cool, stirring from time to time.

Slice each choux pastry across the middle, to form two small containers. The bottom part will lie flat easily, but you may need to adjust the top part by levelling the bottom with a knife.

Place the choux containers onto a serving tray or platter and fill each one with a little custard.

Pour the cream into a small bowl and add the icing sugar. Whip the cream, using an electric beater, and transfer to a piping bag. With a medium or small nozzle, pipe cream onto all the choux.

Top with different kinds of fruit, cut into very small pieces, or with whole berries, trying to combine as many colours as possible for variety.

makes 20–40

tips & variations

You can also fill the bigné just with whipped cream or with chocolate custard. To make chocolate custard, follow the basic recipe for custard, then add 50 g of dark chocolate to the hot custard and stir well until melted.

sushi flowers

Invite your friends over for a sushi party. You can prepare the ingredients beforehand, and then roll up the sushi together, with your favourite fillings, and arrange into pretty flower patterns.

500 g sushi rice
4–6 tablespoons sushi dressing
5 sheets nori seaweed
raw vegetables, thinly sliced (e.g. carrot, cucumber, capsicum)

Cook the rice according to the packet instructions. As soon as all the water is absorbed and the rice is cooked, spoon it into a large mixing bowl so that it cools down quickly.

When the rice is cold enough to be touched add the sushi dressing.

Cut each nori sheet down the middle to make two rectangles.

Place a piece of nori over the sushi mat and then wet your hands (it is good to have a bowl of water on the bench just for this purpose).

Pick up a small handful of rice and press it over the nori, leaving a 2-cm strip of nori visible along the top.

Place strips of one kind of vegetable along the middle of the rice. Roll up using the sushi mat to keep it tight.

As soon as you are sure that your roll is well sealed make a gentle pressure with your fingers over the rolled up sushi mat, with the sushi roll inside, shaping it like a long stick of Toblerone chocolate. Set the sushi triangle aside and start with another piece.

Once all the rice has been used, cut each piece into six, starting from the centre. Display the cut sushi in a circular pattern, to look like a flower.

makes approximately 60 pieces;
dairy free

tips & variations

You can use anything you like as filling, as long as it can be cut into a thin strip. A good Japanese ingredient for sushi is takuan, a bright yellow pickled daikon available in many supermarkets.

biscuits & imaginative projects

what kid doesn't have fun with play dough? Once you are old enough to use real dough, you can make your own biscuits and cookies, and experiment with sugar craft or shaping edible marzipan and fondant flowers. With just a little bit of effort, you will be able to create the most delightful sweet treats. In fact, many of the recipes in this chapter can also be used as edible presents. Most of all, remember to have fun with these recipes. We certainly did!

jam biscuit sandwiches

A classic jam biscuit with a twist: a little 'painting' made from icing on top of each biscuit will show what kind of jam has been used. These are perfect for gifts and fancy tea parties.

500 g frozen sweet shortcrust pastry
assorted jams
1 heaped tablespoon icing sugar
1 teaspoon water
food colouring (for natural food colouring, see Tips & Variations)

Preheat the oven to 180°C.

Roll out the pastry to 3 mm thick and cut into circles with a round cookie-cutter. Place pastry circles on a baking tray lined with baking paper and bake for approximately 8-10 minutes.

Remove from the oven and leave to cool on the baking tray.

Turn half the biscuits over and spread with a little jam (being sure to remember which jams you have used on which biscuits). Top with the remaining biscuits to make biscuit sandwiches.

Place the icing sugar in a very small bowl or teacup, then add the water and stir. Using a toothpick, try to draw some dots on a biscuit. If the icing is too runny, add a little more icing sugar. If it is too thick, add a little more water (half a teaspoon at a time).

Divide the icing into small containers and make each into a different colour: for example, add one drop of green food colouring to the first container, one drop of red to the second, and one drop of orange to the third.

Using a toothpick, start drawing the fruit that represents your chosen jam on the top of the biscuit (e.g. cherries, strawberries, plums, apricots, and so on). After you have drawn the fruit, add some stalks and leaves with the green icing.

Let the icing set overnight before storing the biscuits in an airtight container.

makes approximately 40 biscuits

tips & variations

You can make natural colours by using a little
spirulina powder for the green icing, or saffron
for yellow icing, and berry juice instead of the
water for pink and purple hues. A little runny
jam can also be used to colour icing.

very chocolatey cookies

You will be sure to receive compliments for these cookies, as they smell divine and taste even more scrumptious.

100 g dark chocolate
50 g butter
50 g sugar
1 egg
100 g self-raising flour
1 drop vanilla essence
icing sugar to dust

Preheat the oven to 160°C.

Melt the chocolate with the butter, either in the microwave or in the oven (while the oven is warming up).

Stir the chocolate with a spatula to make sure it is well mixed with the butter, then add the sugar, egg, flour and vanilla essence. You should get a very oily cookie dough.

With a teaspoon, shape 20 small balls, which should each be about the size of a walnut. Roll the balls in icing sugar and then place them onto an oven tray lined with baking paper, making sure that you leave some space in between, as the cookies will flatten during baking. Bake for 18 minutes. Even if the fragrance is irresistible, do let the cookies cool completely on the baking tray before lifting them.

makes 20 biscuits

tips & variations

Add a few chopped hazelnuts or almonds to the cookie dough for a nutty version.

teapot biscuits

If you don't have a teapot cookie-cutter, use the stencil at the back of this book and cut out your biscuits carefully with the tip of a knife. These biscuits look really special.

300 g sweet shortcrust pastry
easy royal icing (see recipe on page 26)
runny icing (see recipe on page 29)
red, blue and green food colouring (optional)

Preheat the oven to 180°C.

Roll out the pastry to 3 mm thick and cut out shapes with a teapot cookie-cutter (or use the stencil at the back of this book). Place them on a baking tray lined with baking paper and bake for approximately 8-10 minutes.

Remove from the oven and leave to cool on the baking tray.

Make the royal icing (see page 26) and use it to fill a piping bag fitted with a small nozzle. Draw the outlines of your biscuits. Set aside for 1 hour to set. Store the rest of the royal icing in the bag, closing it with an elastic band so that it doesn't harden – you will need it later.

Make the runny icing (see page 29) and divide it into three containers. Add a drop of red food colouring to the first to make a pale pink icing; a drop of blue to the second to make a china blue; and a drop of green to the third to make a pastel green.

Using a spoon, carefully drop a little runny icing onto each biscuit, spreading it evenly to cover the entire surface. Use a toothpick to spread the icing smoothly onto the handles and spouts. Leave to set for 2 hours.

Finally, decorate your teapots with patterns (e.g. spirals, flowers, squiggles) using the remaining royal icing.

Let the biscuits dry for 1 hour before serving.

makes approximately 20 biscuits

tips & variations

You can use ready-made royal icing to decorate the outlines, if you prefer. This is available in small easy-to-use tubes from specialist stores and some supermarkets.

crown jewel biscuits

Use a crown-shaped cookie-cutter and make 'precious stones' from glacé fruit to create these impressive-looking biscuits. If you don't have a crown-shaped cookie-cutter, use the stencil at the back of this book and cut out your biscuits carefully with the tip of a knife.

500 g sweet shortcrust pastry
easy royal icing (see recipe on page 26)
runny icing (see recipe on page 29)
yellow or red food colouring (optional)
mixed glacé fruit (red and green cherries, citrus peel) to decorate

Preheat the oven to 180°C.

Roll out the pastry to 3 mm thick and cut out crowns using your crown-shaped cookie-cutter (or the stencil at the back of this book). Place them on a baking tray lined with baking paper and bake for approximately 8-10 minutes.

Remove from the oven and leave to cool on the baking tray.

Make the royal icing (see page 26), use it to fill a piping bag fitted with a small nozzle, and draw the outlines of your biscuits. Set aside for 1 hour to set.

Make the runny icing (see page 29) and, if you like, colour it with a few drops of yellow food colouring.

With a spoon, carefully drop some runny icing onto each biscuit, spreading it evenly to cover the entire surface. Use a toothpick to spread the icing evenly onto the tips of the crowns. Before the runny icing sets, decorate your crowns with rubies, emeralds and topaz jewels made from glacé fruit.

makes approximately 30 biscuits

tips & variations

Using the same recipe, you can also make and decorate other biscuit shapes, like flowers and butterflies. Instead of glacé fruit you can use lollies or chocolate buttons.

meringue Christmas wreaths

This recipe contains a lot of sugar as the meringues are designed to be used as long-lasting Christmas decorations (for the tree or for the house). They will keep for a few weeks without getting soft or crumbly. To test the recipe, we hung some meringue wreaths in our kitchen. They lasted for well over a month and still tasted yummy after that!

1 teaspoon cornflour
340 g icing sugar
2 egg whites
1 pinch salt
1 teaspoon lemon juice

Line a baking tray with baking paper. Using a glass, trace some circles on the baking paper with a pen. Turn the paper upside down, so the pen circles show through but won't touch the meringues. Preheat the oven to 50°C.

Sift the cornflour into the icing sugar and set aside.

Place the egg whites in a mixing bowl and beat with an electric beater until soft peaks form. Keep beating, then add the lemon juice and the sugar, one spoonful at a time until all the sugar is well mixed in and the egg white is shiny.

Spoon into a decorating piping bag and pipe hollow circles onto the baking paper.

Bake for approximately 4 hours, opening the oven every half an hour for a few minutes to make sure no humidity develops. Let the meringues cool down overnight in the open oven.

The next day, hang them on your Christmas tree or around the house with colourful ribbons.

makes approximately 20 wreaths; dairy free, wheat free

tips & variations

If you like, you can decorate the meringue wreaths with red and green runny icing (see recipe on page 29) or by using icing pens. Patterns like holly, stars and snowflakes look very festive and are easy to draw.

Christmas tree biscuits

Wrap these biscuits in small cellophane bags tied with a bow, or arrange them in boxes and tins for original Christmas presents. If you don't have a Christmas-tree cookie-cutter, use the stencil at the back of this book and cut out your biscuits with the tip of a knife.

500 g sweet shortcrust pastry
easy royal icing (see recipe on page 26)
runny icing (see recipe on page 29)
1 tablespoon spirulina powder (or green food colouring)
hundreds and thousands, or other fancy sugar sprinkles to decorate

Preheat the oven to 180°C. Roll out the pastry to 3 mm thick and cut into biscuits with a Christmas-tree cookie-cutter. Place the biscuits on a baking tray lined with baking paper and bake for approximately 8–10 minutes. Leave to cool on the baking tray.

Make the royal icing and use it to fill a piping bag fitted with a small nozzle and draw the outlines of your biscuits. Set aside for 1 hour to set.

Make the runny icing and divide into 3–4 small bowls. Add a different amount of spirulina powder (or green food colouring) to each one to get different shades of green. If you like, leave one bowl with white icing so you can create snowy trees. With a spoon, gently and carefully drop some icing onto each tree, spreading it evenly to cover the entire surface. Make trees with different shades of green, or pure white.

Before the runny icing sets, add some hundreds and thousands or sugar sprinkles to decorate your trees. Let the biscuits set for one day before storing in airtight containers.

makes approximately 40 biscuits

tips & variations

You can also decorate your Christmas tree cookies with ready-made coloured icing pens.

vanilla sugar balls

These lovely, fragrant sugar balls are the homemade alternative to sugar cubes. They look pretty stored in a glass jar, and you can also use them when you have guests over for a tea party.

150 g sugar
1 tablespoon water
1 drop vanilla essence
1 drop red food colouring (optional)

Combine all the ingredients in a bowl. Mix well. Fill a second bowl with water and wet your hands.

Pick up a little bit of the sugar mixture and shape it into a hazelnut-sized ball by passing it from the cupped palm of one hand to the cupped palm of the other a few times. When the ball is sufficiently round, place it on a tray lined with greaseproof paper.

Wet your hands again, if necessary, and repeat until you have used up all of the sugar mixture. Store the sugar balls in a secure and dry place, out of direct sunlight, for at least two days, until the balls are completely dry and hard (you can roll them from time to time to make sure they are drying well all over).

makes approximately 16–18 sugar balls; dairy free, wheat free

tips & variations

Make a batch of white sugar balls, and a batch of different shades of pink for visual effect. The vanilla flavour goes well with most teas, and even with hot milk. If you don't want to use artificial colouring, make pink sugar by adding a little berry juice.

tips & variations

Berries all produce beautiful shades of pink and purple. Saffron or turmeric, dissolved in a little warm water, will produce a yellow dye. You can try to make different flowers. For example, shape five oval petals and attach them together at the base for a frangipani, or use icing cutters to make multi-petal flowers like daisies and dahlias.

marzipan & sugar roses & other flowers

Making sugar flowers is a fun thing to do with a friend who's staying over: you can mould the flowers on the first day, then paint them the next morning.

for the roses

ready-made marzipan or ready-made fondant icing

cornflour to dust

for the pink colouring

100 g blueberries (fresh or frozen)

1 tablespoon lemon juice

1 teaspoon sugar

If possible, wear white clothing so as not to leave specks of coloured material on your roses. Roll the marzipan or fondant icing so that it becomes soft. Take a small piece and press it between your thumb and index fingers to make a small petal. Now roll it up to make the centre of the rosebud. Take another small piece and make another small petal to attach to the base of your rose bud. Make 5-6 more petals and attach them all to the base of your rosebud, making sure that the outer petals are a little bigger than the inner petals. Keep dusting your fingers with cornflour throughout this process, so that your fingers don't get too sticky.

With a pair of scissors, cut the base of your rose so that it stands upright.

Set aside and repeat the process until you have as many roses as you need. Leave to dry overnight.

If you'd like to colour some roses pink, place the berries in a bowl along with the lemon juice and sugar and leave to marinate for a few hours, or overnight. Drain the juice into a separate bowl (and eat the berries – they are delicious like this!).

Using a small brush, paint the roses in different shades of pink (you can do this by applying more or less berry 'paint') and leave to dry overnight.

Store in a dry place until it is time to use them.

dairy free, wheat free

tips & variations

You can use any type of ice-cream you like,
but I found that cream-based ice-creams
work better than fruit sorbets for this recipe.
If you don't want a frozen dessert, you can fill
the cones with homemade custard.

puff pastry cannoli with ice-cream filling

Cannoli are pastry cones filled with custard or chocolate. Cannoli moulds can be bought at good kitchen supply stores.

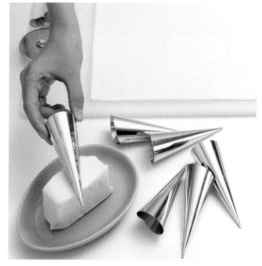

cannoli moulds
butter, for greasing
1 sheet ready-rolled puff pastry
icing sugar to dust

for the filling
3 scoops vanilla ice-cream
3 scoops chocolate ice-cream

Preheat the oven to 180°C.

Grease the outside of the metal cannoli moulds with butter.

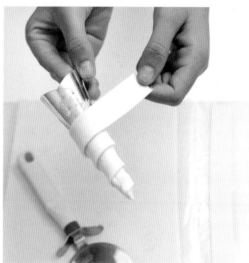

Cut pastry into 6 long strips, about 3 cm thick. Roll each pastry strip in a spiral around a mould. Trim off excess pastry – it can be used for making more cones.

Place the icing sugar on a small plate and lightly dip one side of each pastry cone. Place the cones (sugared side up) on an oven tray lined with baking paper. Bake for 15–20 minutes, or until the cones look golden.

Remove from the oven and leave to cool on their tray before sliding them off their moulds.

When the cones are cold, fill half of them with vanilla ice-cream and half with chocolate ice-cream. You may need to mash the ice-cream a little with a spoon before pushing it inside the cones.

Arrange the cones on a tray and place them in the freezer. Leave to stand in the freezer for at least 1 hour, then serve. The pastry won't freeze, and the ice-cream will be perfect!

makes 6

picnics, lunchboxes & garden parties

eating outside is possibly one of the most fun ways to have a feast. Whether it's a barbecue with your family or a picnic at the beach, eating outside is great because you can run around and play games, rather than just sit around a table. But outdoor eating, especially if it has to be prepared ahead and transported, may take a little planning. So here are a few ideas for your next picnic party, and even for your lunchbox.

picnic puff pastry pizzette

Pizzette are very small pizzas made with puff pastry. They are perfect to take to a picnic because they can be eaten cold, and can be carried in a bag or container without the topping falling off or sticking everywhere.

1 sheet ready-made butter puff pastry
1 tablespoon tomato paste
2 tablespoons grated mozzarella or Edam cheese
1 pinch salt
1 pinch dried oregano

Preheat the oven to 170°C.

Cut the puff pastry sheet into about 16 pieces.

Line a baking tray with baking paper and place the pastry squares on top. Prick each pastry piece with a fork several times to ensure it doesn't puff up too much during cooking. Brush the centre of each square with the tomato paste. If you don't have a pastry brush, use your fingers (as long as they are clean!) – it's a bit like finger painting. Make sure that you leave a little border without tomato paste around the edge of each pizzette.

Top with the grated cheese, a little salt and the oregano.

Bake for 12–15 minutes until the bottom of the pizzette look cooked. Leave to cool down completely before packing them for your picnic.

makes about 16 pizzette

tips & variations

For a special occasion you can cut the pizzette into small discs, flowers or other shapes with cookie-cutters.

fruit sorbet ice-blocks

For a summer garden party, nothing beats an ice-block made with fresh fruit. We love eating these treats after playing sports or other physical activities.

50 g sugar
50 ml water
1 teaspoon lemon juice
400 g fresh fruit (e.g. watermelon, kiwifruit or strawberries)

Place the sugar, water and lemon juice in a small saucepan, bring to the boil and stir until all the sugar has dissolved. Leave to cool.

In the meantime, peel and cut the fruit into small pieces. If using watermelon, or any other fruit with seeds, discard all the seeds first.

Place the fruit and the cooled sweet water into a blender and blend well.

Pour the mixture into ice-block moulds (or plastic cups with ice-cream sticks stuck into the middle of them), making sure not to fill them completely as the mixture will expand during the freezing process. Place into the freezer for at least 6 hours before serving.

makes 6 standard-sized ice-blocks; dairy free, wheat free

tips & variations

When you make watermelon ice-blocks, try adding a few chocolate chips into the moulds: they will look like watermelon seeds. Some fruit (kiwifruit, for example) may be a little sour – simply add a little more sugar. For a creamier ice-block, add a little natural yoghurt to the mixture before blending.

Japanese lunchboxes

These lunchboxes are easy to prepare and perfect for school, picnics, or a quick Japanese meal.

200 g short-grain rice
2 sheets nori seaweed
1 tablespoon vegetable oil
4 eggs
1 pinch salt
1 tablespoon toasted sesame seeds
cucumber slices to decorate (optional)
soy sauce to serve (optional)

Cook the rice according to packet instructions.

In the meantime, cut the nori seaweed into very small strips (about 2 cm long and 0.5 cm wide) with a pair of scissors. Set aside.

Heat the oil in a frying pan over a medium heat. Break the eggs one by one into the pan and add a pinch of salt. Stir the eggs while they are cooking, and keep stirring so that they don't stick to the pan. They should become quite dry. Set aside.

Divide the rice between four small containers that can be closed with a lid and press down well. Top with the scrambled egg and press down to cover the entire surface of the rice. Sprinkle with the nori and sesame seeds and, if you like, decorate with cucumber slices.

This dish is good served at room temperature or cold, but do not refrigerate for too many hours or the rice will become hard. You can serve it with a little soy sauce if you wish.

serves 4;
dairy free, wheat free

tips & variations

With this recipe you can also make simple cut-sushi squares. Press all the rice into a square or rectangular container, cover the rice with the scrambled egg. Compact the rice and eggs down with your fingers. Refrigerate for 1 hour, then cut into small squares that you can lift out. Top each sushi square with cut nori and sesame seeds.

fancy vegetable sticks with broad bean dip

What matters most here is presentation. Collect some small plain jars with lids, wash them well, then measure them and cut the vegetable sticks so that they fit perfectly, standing up, inside the jars.

for the vegetables (choose 3 or more of the following):
carrots (plus lemon juice for soaking)
celery stalks
cucumbers
red capsicums
yellow capsicums
green capsicums
beetroot

for the dip
500 g broad beans (fresh and shelled, or frozen)
2 garlic cloves, peeled
a few fresh mint leaves (optional)
4 tablespoons lemon juice
6 tablespoons extra virgin olive oil
salt and pepper

tips & variations

The vegetable sticks and dip can be prepared the day before, and can also be used for lunchboxes. Any dip is suitable, and you can add a container of mini pita bread, rice crackers or natural corn chips, too.

Cut the vegetables into perfect little straight sticks. If using carrots, soak them in lemon juice so that they will not become brown. Store the vegetable sticks in the fridge, in separate plastic bags or containers, until ready to use.

Make the dip by boiling the broad beans for 5 minutes. Rinse them under cold water then remove their skins (if the beans are large enough. If they are small you may leave the skin on).

In a food processor, blend the beans with the garlic, mint (if using), lemon juice and olive oil. Add salt and pepper to taste.

Store the dip in a container with a lid (or small individual containers with lids, if you have them).

Remove the vegetables from the fridge and arrange them in their jars, one jar for each person.

dairy free, wheat free

potato & vegetable filo parcels

These parcels are super-easy to make. They are also really adaptable – you can eat them warm or cold, indoors or outdoors.

500 g mashing potatoes
1 tablespoon butter
1 tablespoon chopped parsley
200 g frozen mixed vegetables
100 g grated Edam cheese
salt and pepper to taste
6 sheets filo pastry
olive oil to brush

Boil the potatoes until soft. Drain well then, when cool enough to handle, peel and mash them. Add the butter and chopped parsley and mix well.

In the meantime, simmer the mixed vegetables for 5 minutes, then drain and add to the potato mash. Add the grated cheese, then salt and pepper to taste (little by little, and tasting often, so that you don't make it too salty).

Preheat the oven to 180°C.

Place a sheet of pastry on your work surface so that the short side faces you, and brush with olive oil. Place about 2 tablespoons of potato mixture along the short side of the pastry and roll a couple of times, folding in the sides as you go so the edges are sealed. Keep rolling until the parcel looks like a Chinese spring roll. Repeat this process with the remaining filo pastry and filling. Place the parcels on a baking tray lined with baking paper, brush the top with a little water and bake for 20-25 minutes until the pastry is golden.

makes 6

tips & variations

Rather than mixed vegetables, you can simply add corn or peas. You can also substitute the cheese with a teaspoon of curry powder for a mildly spicy version.

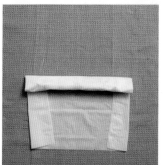

coloured eggs for an Easter picnic

These eggs are great fun to make and they taste and look better than plain hard-boiled eggs. They will be a hit at Easter particularly, but there's no reason you can't make them at any other time.

12 eggs
1 cup brown or red onion skins
1 tablespoon cumin powder
2 cups beetroot cooking water

Place the eggs in a saucepan and cover them with water. Bring to the boil and simmer for 5 minutes. Turn the element off and leave the eggs to cool in their water for 10 minutes. Peel off the shells when the water is lukewarm.

For bright bronze-coloured eggs:
Place the onion skins in a saucepan with a litre of water and bring to the boil. Simmer for 15 minutes, then carefully remove the onion skins with tongs and discard.

Place four shelled hard-boiled eggs into the water, making sure they are completely covered, and simmer for a couple of minutes.

Remove saucepan from the heat, let eggs cool down in the water, then take them out with a spoon and leave to dry on a plate or chopping board.

For yellow eggs:
Place 1 tablespoon of cumin in a saucepan with a litre of water and bring to the boil.

Place four shelled hard-boiled eggs into the water, making sure they are completely covered, and simmer for a couple of minutes.

Remove saucepan from heat and leave to cool in their water, then take them out with a spoon and leave to dry on a plate or chopping board.

For pink eggs:
Pour beetroot cooking water into a bowl.

Place four shelled hard-boiled eggs into the water, making sure that they are completely covered. Let the eggs soak for 30 minutes, then take them out with a spoon and leave to dry on a plate or chopping board.

dairy free, wheat free

tips & variations

You can also use the liquid from a jar
of pickled beetroot to colour the eggs.
Coloured eggs look great whole or
sliced in a salad or in a roll.

lavash salad rolls

Lavash is a flatbread, similar to tortillas, but rectangular in shape. It dries quite quickly so keep it wrapped in a plastic bag when not using it.

4 sheets lavash bread
100 g spreadable cream cheese
100 g lettuce, finely chopped into thin strips
4 tomatoes, chopped
½ cucumber, chopped
2 spring onions, finely chopped

Lay the lavash bread sheets over a work surface so that the largest side faces you, and spread with cream cheese. Sprinkle the chopped lettuce over, leaving a 5 cm space at the end furthest from you (this is needed to seal the rolls). Top the lettuce with the remaining chopped vegetables, making sure that each sheet of lavash has an equal amount of filling. Carefully and tightly roll up each lavash sheet and then cut then in half to make two rolls. Wrap the rolls with plastic food wrap and seal the ends well. These are perfect for a picnic basket.

serves 8

tips & variations

A variety of fillings can be used here: grated cheese, chopped olives, sundried tomatoes, capers, eggs, mayonnaise and rocket are just a few examples. If you can't find lavash bread, use any other type of flatbread.

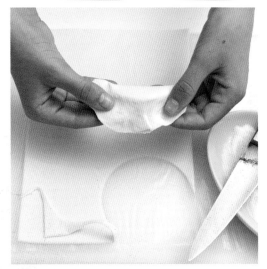

nectarine pasties

Fresh fruit is a healthy and welcome addition to any picnic basket. But if you would like to turn your fruit into something home-baked, filling and light to carry, which is perfect for your next outing, try these simple fruit pasties.

1 large nectarine (or 2 small ones)
2 tablespoons sugar
1 sheet ready-rolled puff pastry
1 tablespoon lemon juice
icing sugar to dust (optional)

Preheat the oven to 175°C.

Cut the nectarine (or nectarines) into 8 segments, removing and discarding the peel and stone.

Sprinkle the sugar on a plate and roll the nectarine slices in it, coating them lightly (don't overdo it, as they only need a little sugar).

Using a round cookie-cutter or a small bowl, cut 8 pastry circles, making sure they are about 2 cm larger than the nectarine slices. Place one slice on one of the pastry discs for a trial. If you can fold it easily into a half-moon shape with the nectarine slice inside, and seal the border well, you have the right-sized disc. Repeat until you have used up all the pastry.

Place the half-moon pasties on a baking tray lined with baking paper and brush with lemon juice. Sprinkle the tops with any sugar left on the plate, (otherwise use a little more sugar, but only just a little sprinkle).

Bake for approximately 20 minutes, until the pastry is puffy and the pasties look golden. Dust the pasties with icing sugar if you wish.

makes approximately 8 pasties

tips & variations

These pasties can also be eaten warm with a bit of cream or custard. You can substitute the nectarines for peaches, plums, apricots, apples or pears.

kids' sangria

This refreshing and fruity drink goes down a treat at a picnic or a disco party. Mix everything directly into a large punch bowl or clean bucket that can fit in the fridge, and serve with a ladle.

1 litre red grape juice
2 litres lemonade
1 teaspoon ground cinnamon
4 red apples
4 oranges
ice cubes to serve

Pour the grape juice and lemonade into the bowl, add the ground cinnamon and stir.

Wash the apples and oranges well, but don't peel them. Cut the fruit into bite-sized chunks, removing the apple cores and the pips that can be removed easily. Place the fruit in the bowl and stir. Refrigerate for at least 2 hours.

Before serving, add some ice cubes. Keep the adults away — if they taste it, they will probably drink it all themselves!

makes over 3 litres; dairy free, wheat free

tips & variations

Decorate with borage flowers and serve in tall glasses with a wooden skewer for each glass, so that your guests can pick up and eat the fruit as well as drink the sangria.

iced peach tea

Try this iced tea if you like a refreshing drink that isn't too sugary or fizzy. You can serve it at your next garden party, or use it to fill your drink bottle for school or outings.

2 teabags (regular or herbal tea, we suggest lemon and ginger or apple)
500 ml boiling water
2 teaspoons sugar
2 tablespoons lemon juice
2 peaches
500 ml cold water

Place the teabags in a jug and cover with boiling water. Add the sugar and lemon juice and stir. Cut the peaches in half, remove stones, then place the fruit in the hot tea.

Leave to stand for about 10 minutes, then remove the teabags.

Add the cold water and refrigerate for at least 2 hours.

Discard the peaches before serving, or eat them if you like – they taste quite good with ice-cream!

makes 1 litre; dairy free, wheat free

tips & variations

If you prefer, use honey instead of sugar. Try experimenting with different-flavoured herbal teas. Fill your drink bottle with iced tea and store it in the freezer overnight for a refreshing drink on a hot school day.

party cakes & desserts

every celebration calls for a beautiful cake. Likewise, every memorable meal needs a stunning dessert to provide that finishing touch. When planning your cakes and desserts, you need to give special attention to taste, look and details. Tailoring your sweet treat specially to the occasion will be sure to earn you some praise. In this chapter there are recipes for all occasions and for all levels of skill. However, they've all got one thing in common: they are all great fun to make!

strawberry yoghurt cake

This is a great cake for beginner bakers: it has only a few ingredients, it does not require much mixing, and it always rises. This is a surefire way to have your guests compliment your baking skills.

butter to grease baking tin
300 g sugar
8 tablespoons strawberry yoghurt
3 eggs
300 g self-raising flour
a few drops red food colouring
icing sugar to dust (optional)

Preheat the oven to 180°C.

Grease a 20 cm non-stick ring cake tin (a round baking tin with a hole in the middle) with butter. If you like you can also place baking paper in the bottom of the tin so that the cooked cake will be easier to remove.

Place the sugar and yoghurt in a mixing bowl and fold together, using a wooden spoon. Continue stirring while you add the eggs, one by one, and then the flour. Mix well, then pour two-thirds into the cake tin.

Add a few drops of red food colouring to the remaining mixture, stir, then pour the now pink batter into the cake tin in a circular pattern. If you like you can make some pink swirls or marbling patterns over the surface of the cake using the spatula or a toothpick.

Bake for 40–50 minutes.

Check if the cake is cooked by inserting a toothpick into the centre. If it comes out clean, the cake is cooked. If not, leave it in the oven for a few more minutes. Carefully remove the cake from the oven, and let it cool down completely before removing it from the tin.

Dust with icing sugar if you wish and serve.

serves 10–12

tips & variations

This cake is also excellent with other yoghurt flavours, like mango, blueberry or banana. In these cases, yellow or blue food colouring can be used.

tips & variations

Make a pineapple mimosa variation by adding canned pineapple pieces to the filling.

mimosa cake

This is a spectacular cake that even younger girls can make. In fact, this is more like a fun assembling project, which can be done in a short time and with spectacular results. It is called 'mimosa' because it resembles the mimosa flower.

300 ml whipping cream
2 tablespoons icing sugar
500 ml custard or crème anglaise
2 x 20 cm round sponge cakes

Using an electric beater, whip the cream until light and foamy. Add the icing sugar and fold in. Add half the whipped cream to the custard or crème anglaise and fold gently. Place both the custard and the rest of the cream in the fridge.

Using a bread knife, carefully remove the entire golden crust from the top, the bottom and the sides of the sponges.

Slice one of the sponge cakes across the middle to make two discs (some ready-made sponge cakes are sold already cut). Place the first disc on a very large serving plate – you will need to leave quite a bit of space around the borders, as the sponge will eventually become a larger dome-shaped cake.

Spread 2 tablespoons of the custard over one of the sponge halves, then top with half the cream. Cover with the other half sponge, and spread the top with the rest of the cream.

Take the other sponge cake, cut into two discs, then cut one disc into a smaller round cake, about 10 cm in diameter.

Place the smaller disc on top of the cake, in the centre, then spread all the remaining custard evenly around the sides and the top of the cake stack.

Cut all the remaining sponge into strips, and then into cubes about 2 cm thick. Assemble the sponge cubes and any crumbs all over the cake, covering its entire surface and shaping it into a dome by pressing the sponge cubes down gently with your fingers. The custard will act as glue, keeping the sponge cubes into place.

Refrigerate for 30 minutes before serving.

serves 8–10

super strawberry trifle

Instead of a baked dessert you could make a fresh strawberry trifle. Serve this in an old-fashioned trifle bowl for a classic look, or choose a funky bowl for a modern version.

for the base
500 g strawberries
juice of 1 lemon
3 tablespoons sugar
½ teaspoon agar-agar powder
1 small sponge cake

for the custard
2 eggs
3 tablespoons sugar
1 tablespoon plain flour
500 ml milk
1 drop vanilla essence

for the topping
300 ml cream
fresh strawberries to decorate

Hull the strawberries, cut into small pieces, then place in a bowl with the lemon juice and the sugar and leave to marinate for a few hours.

Strain and collect 300 ml of juice from marinated strawberries, adding a little water if there is not quite enough liquid.

Place the strawberry juice into a small saucepan, add the agar-agar powder, and bring to a gentle boil and simmer for 3 minutes. Pour into a trifle bowl and leave the jelly to set (about one hour).

Once set, top with the sponge, cut so that it fits the bowl perfectly. Top with the marinated strawberries and any remaining juice. Set aside.

Make the custard by mixing the eggs with the sugar in a saucepan over a medium heat. Add the flour and then, little by little, the milk. Bring to a gentle boil and then simmer until the custard thickens, making sure no lumps form. Turn the heat off, add the vanilla essence, then pour over the strawberries. Let the custard cool down completely.

One hour before serving, whip the cream and spread over the top. Decorate with fresh strawberries and refrigerate until serving time.

serves 8–10

tips & variations

Substitute the fruit to make a raspberry or even a blackberry trifle. Instead of sponge cake you could also use sponge biscuits.

tips & variations

Serve this cake by itself, or with cream
or natural yoghurt. You can also make
an orange version substituting the
lemon zest and juice with orange, and
decorating the cake with orange slices.

a special lemon cake for grandma

Arantxa and I developed this cake especially for both her grand-mothers who love lemony things. Decorating a cake with stencils and letters is an easy and effective way to get your message across.

for the cake

4 eggs

250 g sugar

zest and juice of 1 lemon

200 ml vegetable oil

250 g self-raising flour

oil to grease the baking tin

for the decoration

icing sugar to dust

lemon stencil (see page 128)

1 tablespoon marmalade

thin lemon slices

ribbon

Preheat the oven to 180°C.

Break the eggs into a large mixing bowl. Add the sugar, then beat with an electric beater for about 4-5 minutes, until the mixture is pale yellow. Slow the speed of the beater and add the lemon zest, the lemon juice and, little by little, the vegetable oil. Sift the flour into the mixture and keep beating it on low until well mixed.

Grease a 20-cm non-stick round baking tin with oil, fill with the cake mixture and bake for 40-45 minutes.

To check if the cake is cooked insert a toothpick into the centre. If it comes out clean the cake is cooked, otherwise leave it in the oven for a few more minutes.

When ready, remove the cake from the oven and tip it over onto a serving plate. The bottom of the cake will now become the top, so that it is easier to decorate with icing sugar.

To decorate the cake, cut out the lemon stencil and place it over the cake. You can always add a few more cut-out decorations, or write a message using fridge magnets or stencil letters if you wish.

Dust with icing sugar, then carefully remove the stencils to reveal your pattern. To decorate the border, brush it lightly with marmalade, then apply some very thin lemon slices. Run a ribbon around the border to secure the lemon slices, and tie with a bow. The ribbon and bow can be secured with toothpicks, just remember to remove them before slicing the cake!

serves 10–12; dairy free

raspberry or cherry chocolate cake

A decadent cake for girls who are serious about chocolate and have mastered some basic baking and decorating techniques. Like most chocolate cakes, this one is great for birthdays and special occasions.

for the cake
4 eggs
250 g sugar
200 ml vegetable oil
250 g self-raising flour
2 tablespoons cocoa
1 drop vanilla essence
butter to grease the baking tin

for the filling
2 tablespoons raspberry or cherry jam
100 ml cream, whipped

for the topping
200 g dark chocolate
100 ml cream
fresh raspberries or cherries to decorate

Preheat the oven to 180°C.

Break the eggs into a large mixing bowl, add the sugar and beat, using an electric beater, for 4–5 minutes or until the mixture looks pale yellow. Lower the speed of the beater and add the vegetable oil.

Sift in the flour and cocoa and keep beating it on low until well mixed. At the end, add the vanilla essence.

Grease a round 20-cm non-stick baking tin, or a round silicone cake mould, with the butter. Pour the cake mixture into the baking tin and place in the oven. Bake for approximately 1 hour.

To check if the cake is cooked, insert a toothpick into the centre. If it comes out clean, the cake is cooked. Otherwise, leave it in the oven for a few more minutes.

Remove the cake from the oven (be careful, it will be very hot), wait 5 minutes and then tip the cake over onto a cooling rack, removing it from the tin.

When the cake has cooled down, turn it back over and cut it across the middle into two discs. Spread the bottom disc with a layer of jam, and then with a layer of whipped cream. Arrange the second disc on the top.

Melt the chocolate and cream together to make a ganache (see recipe on page 25), refrigerate for 1 hour, then whip with an electric beater until it doubles in volume. Spoon the ganache into a piping bag and, using a medium or large nozzle, decorate the top of the cake as you fancy. Top with fresh raspberries or cherries to finish.

serves 10–12

tips & variations

All berries look and taste good with this
cake (strawberries, blackberries, blueberries,
redcurrants), and you can also use mixed
berries for a stunning visual effect.

tips & variations

You can substitute the fresh fruit in the topping with 100 g of tropical dried fruit mix (dried bananas, coconut flakes, candied pineapple and papaya chunks and Brazil nuts), or use a mixture of fresh and dried fruit.

sweet & sticky tropical banana cake

This banana cake is so soft and moist that it doesn't really need any topping. But for a special occasion, like Dad's birthday, make an impression by adding fresh tropical fruit on top. Or, because this cake lasts a few days, you could choose a dried fruit topping instead (see Tips & Variations).

for the cake

3 ripe bananas
2 tablespoons lemon juice
½ teaspoon ground cinnamon
200 g sugar
2 eggs
200 ml vegetable oil
200 g self-raising flour
1 pinch salt
1 drop pure vanilla essence
oil to grease the baking tin

for the topping

2 tablespoons honey
2 tablespoons water
1 tablespoon sugar
1 tablespoon icing sugar
fresh tropical fruit (e.g. banana, papaya, pineapple, passionfruit)
coconut flakes to decorate (optional)

Preheat the oven to 180°C.

Peel the bananas and place in a large mixing bowl with the lemon juice and mash with a fork. Add the cinnamon and the sugar and mix with an electric beater set on low.

Add the eggs and the vegetable oil and then, still mixing on a low setting, the self-raising flour little by little. Finally, add a pinch of salt and the vanilla essence.

Oil a round 20-cm non-stick baking tin, or a round silicone cake mould. Cut a disc of baking paper to fit the bottom of the baking tin, if you like, as this will make it easier to flip the cake onto a serving plate afterwards.

Pour the cake mixture into the baking tin and place it in the oven. Bake for approximately 50 minutes.

To check if the cake is cooked, insert a toothpick into the centre. If it comes out clean, the cake is cooked. Otherwise, leave it in the oven for a few more minutes.

When ready, remove the cake from the oven (be careful, it will be very hot) and tip it over onto a serving plate.

Place the honey, water and sugar in a small saucepan and melt over a very low heat.

Quickly pour the sticky topping over the cake and spread well.

serves 10; dairy free

quick & easy apple flan

This flan is so easy and quick to make, and it is sure to be a hit with the adults – especially those who like classic apple pies and cakes.

250 g ready-made butter puff pastry
3–4 large apples
2 tablespoons lemon juice
icing sugar to dust
2 tablespoons apricot jam,
2 tablespoons hot water

Preheat the oven to 180°C.

Roll out the puff pastry to form a large circle, about 25 cm in diameter. Lay the pastry over an oven tray lined with baking paper. Prick lots of holes over the surface of the pastry with a fork.

Peel and core the apples and cut into very thin slices, placing them over the pastry in a circular pattern as you cut them. For best results, work from the edges of the pastry inwards, covering the entire surface of the pastry but leaving a 1 cm border near the ends. Brush the apples with lemon juice and then dust with icing sugar. Bake for 20 minutes.

In a small bowl, thin the apricot jam with the hot water. Carefully remove the flan from the oven and brush the top with the apricot jam, then place back in the oven for another 5 minutes. Serve hot or cold, with cream, custard or ice-cream.

serves 6

tips & variations

You can also dust this flan with ground cinnamon before baking, or add some almonds or glacé cherries to the topping.

fruit agar-agar jelly cake

Agar-agar is a seaweed-based product that does not contain sugar or fat. It sets very easily, making it perfect for tall and stable jelly cakes.

**2 x 400 ml cans fruit in syrup (e.g. fruit salad, peaches, pears
    or apricots, but avoid pineapples as they don't set well in jellies)**
1 tablespoon sugar
2 teaspoons agar-agar powder
a few drops of lemon juice
2 punnets blackberries or blueberries

Drain the canned fruit and collect the syrup. Add enough water to the syrup to make up 1 litre of liquid. Place the liquid in a saucepan with the sugar, agar-agar and lemon juice. Bring to the boil and simmer for 3 minutes, stirring often.

Arrange half the fruit in a 2-litre jelly mould. Cover with half the agar-agar mixture (this will be hot, so be careful). Arrange the remaining fruit, trying to alternate the berries with the canned fruit to achieve an interesting colour variation. Cover with the remaining agar-agar mixture. Let the jelly cool down to room temperature and then place in the fridge for at least 1 hour.

Before serving, tip the jelly mould over a serving plate. Serve by itself or with ice-cream.

serves 12; dairy free, wheat free

tips & variations

The berries will add a light purple colour to the jelly, which looks great. For a redder jelly, use a can of pitted cherries, and for a clear jelly avoid red fruit.

ice-cream bomb

Making cakes with ice-cream is easy, and no baking is required, so it is a perfect project for beginners and those who love frozen desserts.

2 litres chocolate ice-cream
2 litres vanilla ice-cream
1 x 400 ml can pitted cherries
ice-cream chocolate sauce to decorate (optional)

Line a Pyrex glass or metal bowl with plastic food wrap, making sure to leave plenty of overhang. This will help you remove the finished ice-cream bomb from the mould.

Let the chocolate ice-cream melt just enough to become workable with a spoon, then transfer it to the bowl, covering all the sides and leaving a large empty space in the middle. Basically you are trying to make a chocolate bowl inside your bowl! Refrigerate for 1 hour, making sure from time to time that the ice-cream is sticking to the borders. If your chocolate 'bowl' collapses, restore it with the back of a spoon.

When frozen, fill with half the vanilla ice-cream, once again covering only the sides, and leaving a small space in the centre. Refrigerate for 1 more hour.

Drain the cherries and discard the juice (or you can keep it for making pink icing, or for adding to desserts or drinks). Mix the remaining ice-cream with the cherries until it becomes pink and fill the remaining hole in your ice-cream bomb. Level well with a spoon and refrigerate for at least 2 hours. Before serving, tip the bowl onto a serving plate and release the ice-cream. Remove the plastic food wrapping and, if you like, top with some ice-cream chocolate sauce.

serves 12–14; wheat free

tips & variations

You can obviously use any ice-cream flavour you like here — the important thing is to have at least three layers of colour. Instead of cherries you can use a can of blackberries or plums.

tips & variations

Using royal icing, you can also glue lollies to your house. Or, using marzipan, mould a chimney, a letterbox or figurines (like a snowman). Use ready-made icing and icing pens instead of royal icing and runny icing.

cookie house

This is a lovely project for Christmas, and one that most adults would love to have the patience and time to make.

500 g ready-rolled sweet shortcrust pastry
icing pens and ready-made icing
easy royal icing (see recipe on page 26)
runny icing (see recipe on page 29)
food colouring (optional)
sponge or other cake to support the inside of the house
icing sugar to dust (if making a snowy house)

Preheat the oven to 175°C and line a baking tray with baking paper.

Cut the pastry using the three biscuit house stencils at the back of this book and bake for 15 minutes, or until it looks golden on top and light brown underneath. Leave the pieces in the oven with the door open to dry out and cool down. Make the royal icing and the runny icing.

Laying the pastry pieces flat, draw the outlines of the door and window frames first with royal icing (it is easier if you draw a plan on a piece of paper first). Wait 1 hour to make sure that the outlines are dry and then colour in with the runny icing. Set aside and let the icing dry overnight.

Store the leftover royal icing in the piping bag closed with a rubber band and the runny icing in an airtight container. You will need to use them again the next day when you assemble the house.

To assemble the house, first lay the four walls on a flat surface to measure the area of your house.

Cut a piece of sponge cake as big as the perimeter and as tall as the walls. Add a bit of runny icing to the back of the walls to act as glue and stick the walls to the cut cake.

Using a small or medium nozzle, pipe royal icing through the joints of the walls to cover any gaps. Remember that the walls may not be perfectly aligned because the biscuit will have grown and changed shape while baking. Once the walls are stable, pipe some royal icing on the borders and attach the roof. Complete by piping a strip of royal icing where the two roof biscuits join. You can also dust the house with icing sugar to create a snow effect.

conversion tables

The following amounts have been rounded up or down for convenience. All have been kitchen tested.

METRIC TO IMPERIAL

10-15g	½oz
20g	¾oz
30g	1oz
40g	1½oz
50-60g	2oz
75-85g	3oz
100g	3½oz
125g	4oz
150g	5oz
175g	6oz
200g	7oz
225g	8oz
250g	9oz
300g	10½oz
350g	12oz
400g	14oz
450g	1lb
500g	1lb 2oz
600g	1lb 5oz
750g	1lb 10oz
1kg	2lb 3oz

50-55ml	2fl oz
75ml	3fl oz
100ml	3½fl oz
120ml	4fl oz
150ml	5fl oz
170ml	6fl oz
200ml	7fl oz
225ml	8fl oz
250ml	8½fl oz
300ml	10fl oz
400ml	13fl oz
500ml	17fl oz
600ml	20fl oz
750ml	25fl oz
1 litre	34fl oz

Please note:
1 pint in the UK = 16fl oz
1 pint in the USA = 20fl oz

OVEN TEMPERATURES

Celsius	Fahrenheit	Gas Mark
120°	250°	1
150°	300°	2
160°	325°	3
180°	350°	4
190°	375°	5
200°	400°	6
220°	425°	7

BAKING TIN SIZES

Common square and rectangular baking pan sizes:

20x20cm	8x8 inch
23x23cm	9x9 inch
23x13cm	9x5 inch loaf pan/tin

Common round baking pan sizes:

20cm	8 inch
23cm	9 inch
25cm	10 inch

Note: baking paper = non-stick baking parchment.

TABLESPOON MEASURES

In New Zealand, South Africa, the UK and the USA 1 tablespoon equals 15ml. In Australia 1 tablespoon equals 20ml.

glossary

Agar-agar: a setting agent made from seaweed, found in flake or powder form, which can be used instead of gelatine to make jellies. Available from Asian food stores.

Bain-marie: a gentle cooking method achieved by placing a pot or bowl over another pot filled with simmering water. Bain-marie is commonly used to melt chocolate.

Bigné (beeg-NEY): choux pastry cases filled with cream, chocolate or custard.

Bocconcini (bok-on-CHEE-nee): small bite-size balls of mozzarella cheese.

Butter puff pastry: a flaky pastry that can be used in sweet and savoury baking, and is available ready-made and frozen from the supermarket.

Choux pastry (shoo): light pastry used mostly for eclairs and profiteroles. It is available in most supermarkets, ready to fill with cream and/or custard.

Fondant icing: ready-made rolling icing, available from the supermarket.

Ganache (gan-ASH): a sweet spread made with chocolate and cream that is used to decorate cakes, cupcakes and biscuits.

Italian butter icing: a soft icing made with butter, sugar and egg whites.

Lavash: a flat rectangular bread, similar to a tortilla, that is available from most supermarkets and Asian food stores.

Marzipan: a paste made from almond and sugar used to decorate cakes, available from the supermarket.

Nori: sheets of dried seaweed used for sushi rolls, and in Japanese and Korean cuisine, available from most supermarkets and Asian food stores.

Petit fours (peh-tee-FOR): small, decorated sweet or savoury treats, usually served at parties and special occasions.

Rolling icing: see fondant icing.

Rose water: a rose-flavoured water used to make sweets and confectionery, available in many Asian, Middle Eastern and specialist food stores.

Royal icing: an egg white-based icing that is soft to start with, so it can be piped directly onto cakes and other sweet preparations. It sets hard like a meringue, and is often used to decorate wedding and birthday cakes.

Runny icing: an egg white-based icing that is quite runny to start with, so it can be used for smooth icing coverings. It sets hard like a meringue, and is often used to decorate biscuits and cupcakes.

Spirulina (spih-roo-LEE-nah): a green powder made from freshwater seaweed. A common ingredient in fruit smoothies, it can also be used as a natural green food colouring.

Sushi dressing: a rice vinegar dressing available in supermarkets and Asian food stores.

Sweet shortcrust pastry: a butter-based sweet pastry used to make biscuits and pies, available as ready-made and frozen from the supermarket.

Verrine: food layered and served in a glass or a small glass bowl, and generally used for starters or desserts.

index

These symbols indicate:
- 🦢 dairy-free recipe
- 🍃 wheat-free recipe

acknowledgements

A big thank you to all the staff at New Holland Publishers, to project manager Christine Thomson, editor Louise Russell, proofreader Frances Chan and designer Sarah Elworthy.

Also Arantxa and I would like to thank photographer Shaun Cato-Symonds for being so great to work with, and all the people who helped us with the photo shoots: Claire, Frances, Morgan and Patricia, who volunteered in the kitchen, and to all the beautiful girls and boys who modelled alongside Arantxa: Bijou, Emily, Max, Patricia, Quinn, Sophie and Yana.

Finally, thank you Peter for always being there for me.

credits

Ceramics: Morgan Haines, Frances Chan and the author's private collection.
Cupcake paper cups: Epicure Trading

stencils & patterns

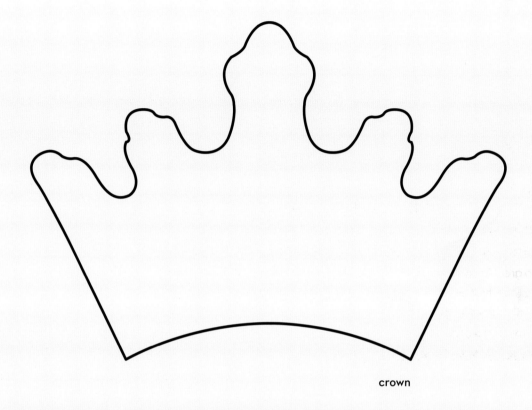

crown

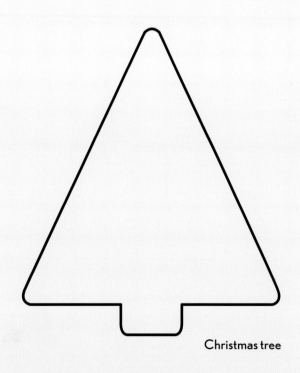

Christmas tree

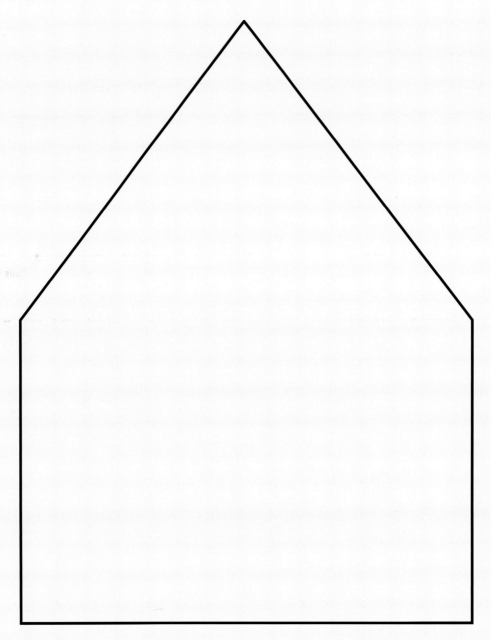

cookie house front/back

cookie house walls x2

cookie house roof x2

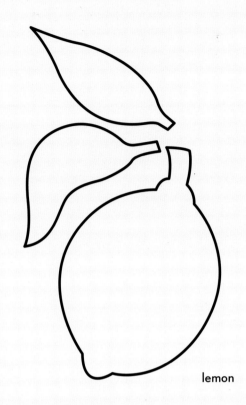

lemon

teapot